A MILLENNIAL'S GUIDE TO BRANDING

CANDICE LEIGH KING

Acknowledgments

I want to thank the previous generations for encouraging us to build on your roofs. Thank you to Generation X for believing that we, the Millennials, can achieve greatness and telling us we can do so. Your support and invigoration has set us up for success. You are the reason behind our aspirations.

To my parents, Jane and Jerome Schofield. The ones who funded my education. Thank you not only for your financial and emotional support, but for believing in me enough and trusting me to experiment with your livelihood, your business. Your brand.

A sincere thank you to Vega School of Branding, my lecturers and my peers for teaching me everything I know about branding and setting the bar high. Thank you for giving me the tools needed to explore branding and the freedom to make it my own.

Lundi Coetzee and Kate Maxwell, thank you for being so patient with me and laying such a firm brand management foundation.

To Clive Greenstone, you opened my eyes to so much. Thank you for teaching me to be critical.

Steffie Betts, your continuous support is greatly appreciated.

Lastly, to my husband, Jonathan King. You've seen it all, been part of it all and loved it all. You've supported me in all my failures and successes, and you've encouraged me to take my aspirations further. Thank you for reading every email, letter, message, Instagram caption, Facebook status and every single book of mine. Your faith in me is inspiring.

A Millennial's Guide to Branding
Candice Leigh King

Content Page

INTRODUCTION Building an Empire	09
CHAPTER ONE Bigger than a profit	11
CHAPTER TWO Planting a seed	15
CHAPTER THREE Getting Rooted	19
CHAPTER FOUR Taking a Stand	23
CHAPTER FIVE Branching out	27
CHAPTER SIX The fruit of your brand	33
CHAPTER SEVEN Appetiser	37

INTRODUCTION
BUILDING AN EMPIRE

When I was developing my own brand, the first thing I thought I needed was a powerful name and logo (even though this wasn't what I was taught). So, I came up with a brand name, created social media accounts, a website and a blog to market what I was doing. I knew what I wanted. In fact, I wanted to do so much, but that wasn't the problem. The problem was how it would all piece together. Well, with each new idea, the name of my business changed and by the time the brand was two-years-old, the name had changed four times. The whole thing was a mess, but I kept learning and experimenting. I practiced building brands day in and day out. I wrote a silly amount of brand strategy documents on made up brands and business ideas. During this process, I was developing my branding philosophy. Since, I've put this method to the test and the outcomes have been great. Every brand building challenge I've tackled has been a success.

Even after all my studies, tens of projects and completing a degree in branding, it wasn't enough to master the subject, and that's when I realised that branding is changing rapidly, therefore methods used to create brands need to change too. I've realised that the subject of branding is going through a revolution, and that's because we; the branders, the entrepreneurs, the opportunists, want more.

We want to see the world transformed by our vision. We want to bring environmental cures to Earth and we want to see poverty broken. We don't only want to be business owners, we want to be global leaders, and we believe that through our brands, we can do just that.

In the past, we've witnessed multimillion dollar corporations practicing corrupt business and covering these operations through whitewashing and greenwashing. We've seen how many organisations portray an image of themselves that doesn't correspond to the brands' cores. These brands are known as unhealthy and unethical. While they are providing consumers with fancy products all while filling their own pockets, the long term impact is frightening. Frightening not for environmental concerns only, but in that consumers are smarter, there are more options (competition) than ever before, and the heart of the world is turning. Communities want to support healthy brands, but in most cases, the traditional branding methods have failed to create organic and genuine brands founded on good intentions.

We are doing more. We are inventing businesses that have never been done before. We're tackling issues that weren't a problem before. Therefore, we need a new branding strategy that supports and encourages the Millennials' businesses.

This book is a Millennial's guide to building a healthy brand that will transform the business world from the inside out.

① Bigger than a profit

I have two questions for you. For some of us, it's a question we've pondered over a hundred times, while for a handful of us maybe once or twice in our lives.

Who am I and what was I created for?

For many of us, the first answer is our names. Then, we usually go on to sharing more details about ourselves like where we were born, our current place of residence, our hobbies and our jobs. Further information would be about our family or people we spend most of our time with. Our education, the languages we speak, our favourite foods, holiday and travel destinations. Our experiences, our culture and the person we've fallen in love with. However, these things are only the results of who we are and what we were created for. Who we are is much, much greater than that.

If we strip ourselves to the core and we pull off these layers "that make us who we are and what we're created for" what do we have left?

If your answer is "nothing" then you've based your identity on external circumstantial matters, which provide a weak foundation for a strong, functional person to thrive. Our identity has to be determined by something bigger than our circumstances and bigger than our possessions.

This is the same with businesses all around the world. The ones that thrive during a recession or economic crisis are the ones that haven't based their identity on their products, services or customers. They base their identity on their essence which extends far beyond that which the market sees. It extends beyond their profits, services and business plan. Essence is the pure reason for mere existence, which powers vision, dreams and purposes.

Companies that understand this are not in business for insignificant gain like finance. Such companies are in business to leave a legacy and to transform the world with their purpose using their services and products as a tool to establish their legacy. These are the organisations that inspire, lead and restore. These organisations are driven by their passion to see their vision in fruition.

This book is not about how to make money. It's so much more than that. This book is a guide on how to create a strong and ethical brand that shapes our world. The end result of your business being healthy and genuine is, of course, handsome profits.

Throughout this guide, I'm going to show you examples and models I created for one of South Africa's leading insurance brokerages, JSib. This way, you'll be able to take the examples and models given, and apply them to your own business and brand.

For JSib, their essence determines their purpose, and their purpose hones JSib's essence. It is JSib's purpose that gives the company greater meaning and adds value to the community.

A healthy business profits from using their products, services and sub-brands as a means to achieving their purpose, and uses the profits earned to invest in the company's purpose.

Purpose Driven Business Model

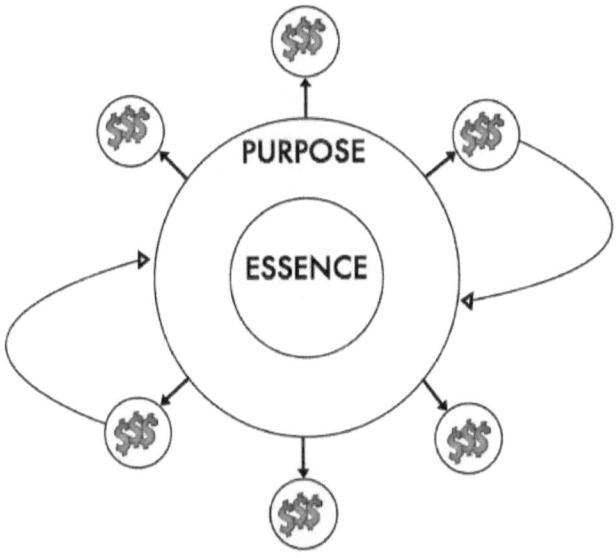

I want to encourage you to really question your motives and discover the reason behind your new venture. Your business has so much more potential than gaining a profit. Your business idea has the power to change the way businesses operate and it has the power to become a legacy and monetise while doing so. For a moment, I want you to look beyond monetising and allow the true purpose of your company to take you to the next chapter, but before you realise your company's purpose, you first need to discover your essence.

2
Planting a Seed

Knowing our purpose and defining our brand's calling is difficult without first uncovering the true meaning to the question: What was I created for?

In this question lies your company's essence, which is also your company's seed; the birthing of your brand. It is the reason it was born. You should be able to summarise your company's essence into one word.

For example, JSib was created for relationship. The brokerage is fully aware that meaningful relations connect them to the company's greater purpose, and this greater purpose is to "humanise before we monetise". Uplifting humanity and making a difference in the business world is the brokerage's calling. JSib's purpose is not only to influence business owners to do what is humane and civil, but to be humane. Being humane gives the corporation no other option but to act humanely.

The result of this is a healthy business and the outcomes of a healthy, ethical business are major profits which are then sown into the purpose as shown in the Purpose Driven Business Model.

It's worth mentioning that the seed or essence is not your business idea. The essence comes before your business idea. Essence is an ethical reason for the creation of your brand.

Following, is an example of what JSib's business seed or essence looks like and how this extends into the brand's purpose.

JSib's Essence

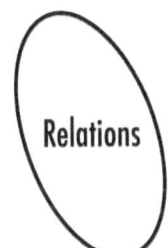

JSib's Purpose

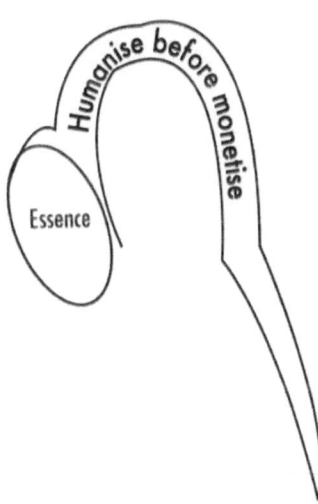

JSib's purpose encourages respectable and healthy relationships making the essence and purpose of the brand work hand in hand. As in this example, your essence and purpose should enrich and strengthen one another.

Using this example, you'll be able to uncover your brand's unique essence and purpose. In order to be sure, write down a few terms that you believe are most suitable for your company. Follow this with a few statements that can be defined as an ethical purpose. Once you've done this, ask yourself if they enrich each other, build on one another and if your essence drives your purpose.

③ Getting Rooted

A healthy seed, produces a healthy sprout. And a healthy sprout becomes a healthy root system that securely holds the plant even during bad weather conditions. This is the same with brands. If the company is created out of good intentions, its roots will be strong enough to anchor the entire organisation no matter the circumstances or market condition.

Out of an ethical essence, an incorruptible purpose forms which produces a succession of steadfast values. These values are your brand's roots.

In order to recognise your organisation's values, I suggest pinpointing a core value that can be found in a number of different values. A core value supports and edifies minor values.

When I was developing JSib's identity, I worked closely with the founder, Jerome Schofield. I studied him, asked questions and really got to know his heart personally and his heart for his company. After a few months, I realised that I wasn't developing a brand identity. I was simply drawing out the gold that was already there. This was how I was able to define JSib's core value: honesty. This value was evident in all of Schofield's business methods, and with honesty being at his core, acting out in any other way would be against his nature and against the nature of the brand. In simple terms, apple seeds produce apple trees. You can't get an apple out of an orange tree. No matter how hard you try, you can't force an apple to grow. You can paint the oranges to make them look like apples, but the moment customers take a bite, they will soon realise that you are in fact producing oranges. The same idea goes for businesses. You'll never produce sincere values that later become a healthy brand, if a virtuous essence isn't already in place.

Lastly, a strong set of values is what keeps the company from swaying. There will be moments when your company is put under pressure, but it will be a healthy root system that keeps the company from buckling into unethical business practices.

On the following page, there's a diagram of JSib's value system. The brokerage has a succession of values, and they recognise that these values cannot be something they do or even live by. These values have to be who they are. This way, the organisation has no other option but to act and react in fulfillment of their values.

A Healthy Brand's Value System

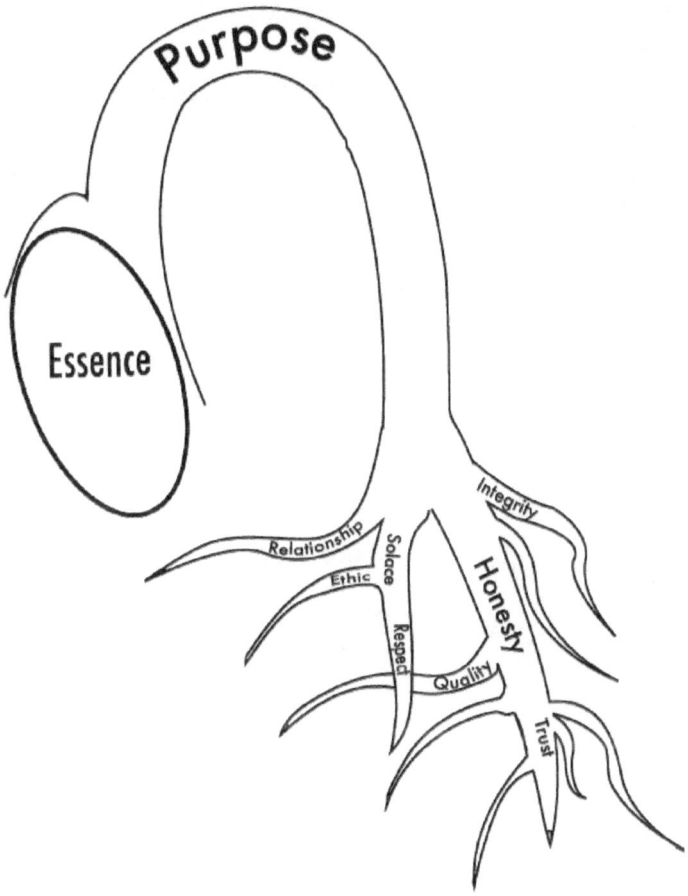

The insurance brokerage acknowledges that each of these values carry weight, and some, more than others. For example, meaningful relationships connect JSib to a community that's ever growing and it is in this community that they find themselves working towards their purpose. Another one of JSib's values is solace, as it compels them to help and correct the situations they have the authority and influence to do so. This is where their main value of honesty is essential as it empowers JSib to act justly and accordingly.

These three aspects: essence, purpose and values form the core of a brand and it is the core that makes your brand who and what it is. This core is a brand's identity which can be expressed in many different ways.

I'll get more into this in the following chapters.

Your core will be the force behind what you do. It also determines how your organisation will respond to certain situations and how it deals with its customers, partners and employees.

Core Identity

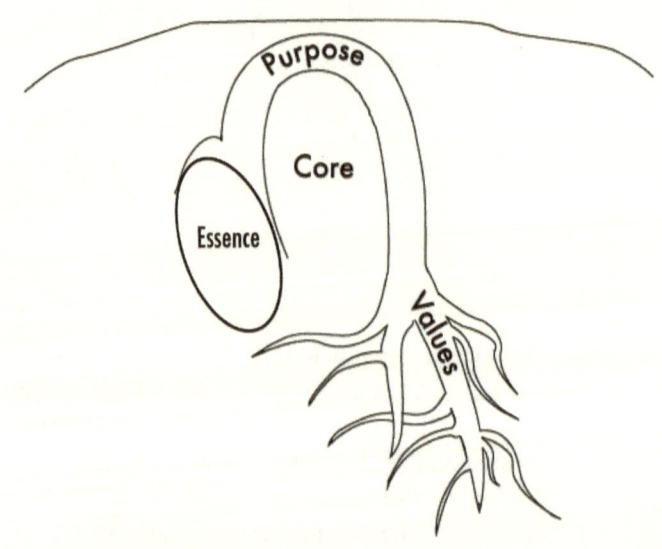

4
Taking a Stand

In 2017, I began to uncover JSib's brand. I discovered that the 28-year-old company was more than a simple acronym that stood for Jerome Schofield insurance brokers. I learnt that the business stood for much more and I wanted to reveal it. I also wanted the company to have a clear, clean and consistent position in the marketplace, and I wanted the company to live out a clear, clean and consistent message that represented what it stood for. In order to do this, however, it took a few weeks of asking the same questions differently. Taking this into account, I realised that studying JSib's founder and his motives weren't enough. I had to ask Schofield the same question using different words.

That's what this section is about. It's redefining and refining after your core has been defined. This section acts as the pillar of your brand. It's the trunk of the tree, and without it, your business will lack in internal structure.

Unlike your brand's core, this aspect will be visible to the public through the functioning of your business. In other words, customers might not see your essence, purpose or values, but they will certainly recognise them by what you stand for or endorse.

The best way to understand the pillar of your brand, is to write a list of that which your brand stands for. A few of your brand's values should reappear. This shows the aspects of your brand are conjoined giving us a clear idea of your brand.

Brand's Pillar

Relationship

Nobility

Solace

Impartiality

Purpose

Essence

Values

⑤
Branching Out

Trees are a great metaphor to use when building a brand. Trees have the whole growing process down! They just seem to know exactly what to grow, when to grow and how to extend.
When it comes to cultivating a stalk, all plants will only do so if it's firmly rooted in the ground. Most trees also don't yield branches unless the trunk and roots are strong enough to bear the weight.

Nature is a beautiful and, sometimes, incomprehensible aspect of life. When uninterrupted, it grows extraordinarily, and when it is interrupted by unforeseen circumstances, instead of withering, nature will restrain growth in order to bear more fruit when the conditions have turned. This is because nature grows in the right way.

In this chapter, we are going to look at our brand's branches.

For many in the business world, branches or branching out would mean to expand, and expand in the sense of a new office, agency, store, headquarters and so on. However, in this guide, branching out is a term used when looking at a brand as physical entities.

Since the brand's values are in place and a stem or trunk has formed and it's stable enough to branch out in other areas, we'll look at your brand as three different aspects. These aspects are termed 'branches' and are important features that compose your brand. These three branches are formed when we look and describe your brand as the following:

1. Your brand as a person
2. Your brand as an organisation
3. Your brand as a symbol

In the same way that the core of the brand is recognised through the company's stance, both the core and the stance should manifest and be recognisable when looking at the brand as these three physical aspects.

Your brand as a person
If your company was a person, what kind of person would it be? What type of friends does this person have? What sort of relationships does he/she have? Who does this person associate with?
For example, amongst friends, JSib is known as the know-how; the intellectual, the one with wisdom. She gives great advice, therefore she's the advisor in the group and has the responsibility of influencing ethically. She is highly valued, and is trusted deeply by those she associates with.

The more you distinguish about your brand as a person, the better. This doesn't only stimulate your brand's voice, but it helps you to understand the type of person you'd one day like to employ and even the partnerships and customers you might like to have in the future.

Ask yourself other questions like: where does he/she spend their

money and time? What sort of job does this person have? What are his/her hobbies? What sort of personality does he/she have? How about this person's skills and responsibilities? What country does this person come from and what languages can she/he speak?
Develop this person well enough to write a CV, or create a Facebook account for them (don't actually do this though; it would be a little weird).

Your brand as an organisation
Think of your brand as a unique group of people. What group do you believe would edify your brand or represent your brand well? Are they a global group of people or are they local? It could be a group of business-know-hows, a band or an NGO. Think about the culture and values of this group. Focus on the group's attributes and not necessarily what they do. Look at what they mean to their followers and the message they portray.

Again, take time documenting your ideas, and once you've done so you can turn your answers into a paragraph that will help others understand your enterprise.

Your brand as a symbol
More than a logo or a sign, what does your brand represent? What does it symbolise? Use metaphors to describe your brand. Think of your brand's heritage and how it became what it is today. Look at your brand's roots and reflect on these values. Are any of these values represented in the brand's stance and are any of these values mentioned in other areas of your brand's identity? What metaphors can you use to describe these values?
Think about what your brand means to the community and only after you've done this, look at visual imagery. Is there anything or any imagery that embody your brand's identity? Is this imagery seen often or is it completely new?

For example, to the community, JSib is a symbol of assurance, and with assurance comes peace and security. Hence the peace dove in their logo.

Following, is a diagram of a brand core identity manifesting itself through these three aspects which is the brand's extended identity.

Brand Extended Identity Model

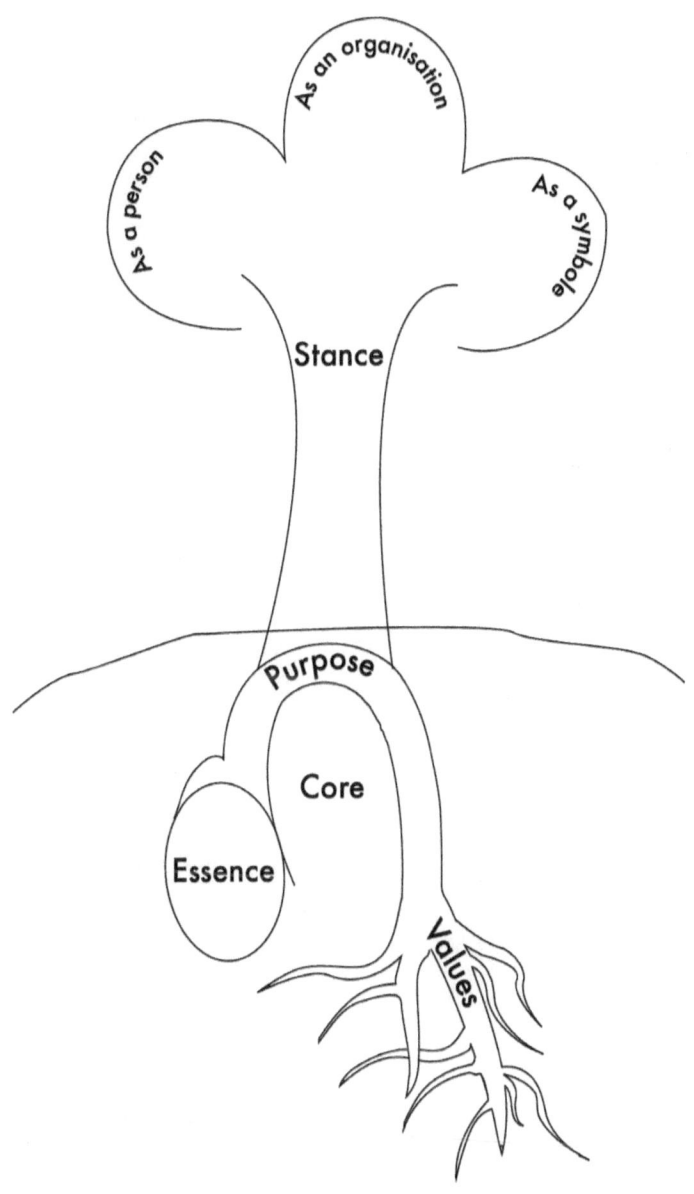

6
THE FRUIT OF YOUR BRAND

Now that we have a clear understanding of the brand, we can discuss products, services, brand extensions, sub-brands and new business ventures. Many branding gurus like David Aaker, whom I hold in high esteem, added this section to their brand as part of one of its branches (its extended brand identity). Many will incorporate the brand's services and/or products as part of the brand's extended identity. This has been one of the biggest challenges within the branding community, as branders establish companies on ideas when ideas develop, change and even die. This leaves us with an empty basket.

While I do regard services and products as a type of extended manifestation of the brand's identity, I don't, however, regard it as part of the brand's identity. A brand's services/products are its fruit, which is experienced by the market. Again, let's consider an apple tree. Whether or not it produces fruit, it will still be an apple tree, because of its seed. Whether or not your business has a product or a service, it should still be a brand, because of its essence. This way, your brand will be able to express its core (its essence, purpose, and values) through many different avenues. Not only this, but it's unlikely that your brand will depend on the market conditions for it's success.

Your brand's new business ideas, known as the fruit, can be anything the brand does to achieve the brand's purpose. From its products and services, brand extensions and sub-brands, these are all considered fruit. These are the by-products of an ethical brand. These are the means to achieving your (business) purpose. And if you're anything like me, you'll pick up new objectives and dreams along the way. This is the result of a strong and healthy brand identity that empowers great and successful purposes.

Brand Service and Product Model

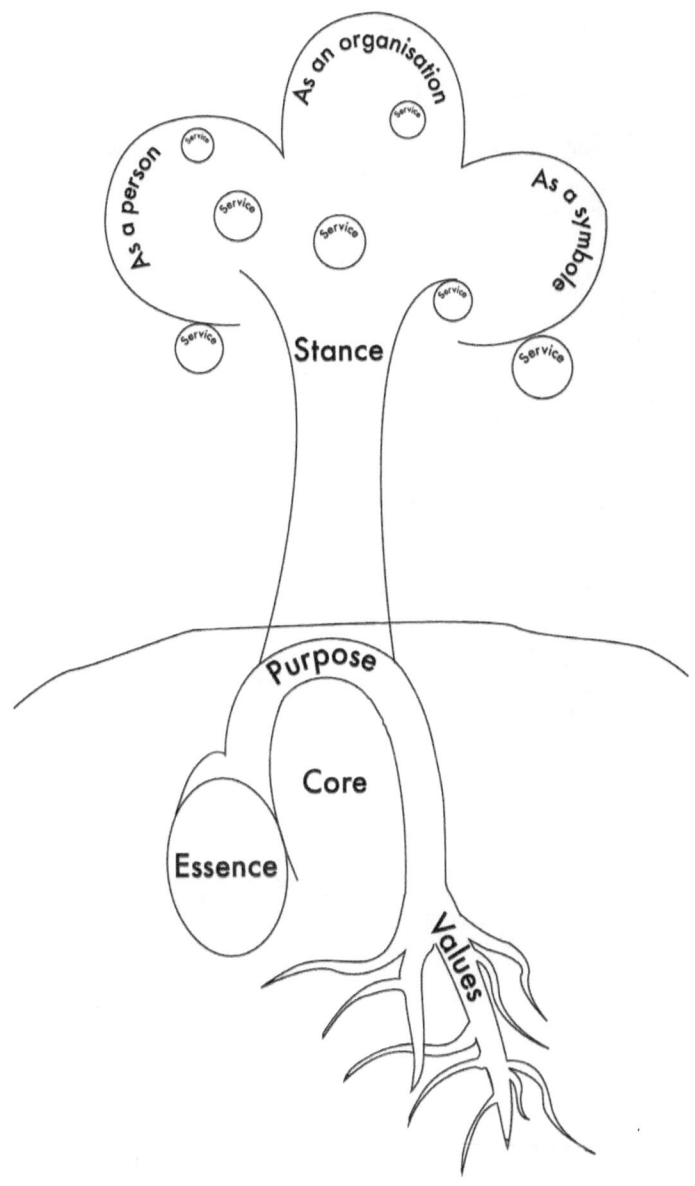

7
Appetiser

In the past, branding was centred around the consumer and the type of service or product it provides. When it came to marketing these new products, the goal was getting consumers to choose their product or service over another instead of determining the best and most suitable strategy to achieve the business purpose. In doing so, providing consumers with another choice.

Marketers also have difficulties marketing these brands based on their identity, as many are built on unethical or unworthy intentions. Therefore, marketers would rather not market these companies based on their true brand identity. This is the reason behind many companies having no option but to be painted green and white, portraying an image that is fabricated.

In many cases, new business ideas have forced companies to consider changes in the brand and the brand identity. In my understanding, something we do doesn't and shouldn't change who we are. Our identity isn't determined by our actions. Our actions are determined by our identity.

Consider the character of a gentle person. This person would be regarded as acting out of nature by displaying signs of aggression and violence. In the same way, a business would operate outside its identity by practicing unethical business. That is only if the company was founded ethically. If founded unethically, healthy operations would be artificial or forced. It's worth mentioning that acting out of character isn't desiring new business or having new ideas. Acting out of nature is going from ethical motivations and practices to unethical motivations and practices. In other words, our intentions turn from pure to greed.

Take CazFit for example, a fresh, up and coming fitness brand. Caroline, the founder, had a completely different outlook when we were developing her brand. Her essence was joy and this inspired the brand's purpose: empowering women to pull off any broken mask by teaching them to first delight in who they are created to be, then to delight in what they can achieve.

A powerful objective, as mentioned above, can be achieved through many different services and products. Caroline chose to first focus on building inner joy through fitness as it creates confidence and joy. With this essence and purpose, she could also establish a school, a restaurant or even go into clothing. Her brand, CazFit and the brand's identity won't be forced to change in the future when considering new business ventures or as I see it: new strategies to achieve the dream.

I want to encourage you to keep your brand pure. Doing this, there will be no reason to recreate a brand image or identity, as your image should be an exact representation of your brand's identity. Creating your brand's identity can be tedious and it is a mountain of work, but in defining your brand, you'll have a better understanding and vision of that which comes next: marketing.

ABOUT THE AUTHOR

Candice Leigh King

After qualifying with a BA Degree in Creative Brand Communications specialising as a Copywriter, Candice Leigh King began her real brand building journey. She spent the next four years travelling around the world as an educator, missionary and author, all while developing her own branding philosophy and putting it into practice. She's rebranded companies, branded new companies and founded an NPO. Currently, she's the Head Educator at one of the top British International Schools in Laos where three of her books will be published in both English and Lao.

PERSONALLY CONNECT

- facebook.com/candy.leigh.king/
- @candy_leigh_king
- @leighking_candy

www.ingramcontent.com/pod-product-compliance
Lightning Source LLC
Chambersburg PA
CBHW031555210526
45464CB00003B/1307

9 7 8 1 7 2 3 9 3 0 3 3 1